INSANELY PRACTICAL LEADERSHIP

STUDY GUIDE

Copyright © 2024 by Stephen Blandino

Published by AVAIL

All rights reserved. No portion of this book may be reproduced, stored in a retrieval system, or transmitted in any form or by any means—electronic, mechanical, photocopy, recording, scanning, or other—except for brief quotations in critical reviews or articles, without prior written permission of the author.

Unless otherwise specified, all Scripture quotations are taken from the Holy Bible, New Living Translation, copyright © 1996, 2004, 2015 by Tyndale House Foundation. Used by permission of Tyndale House Publishers, Inc., Carol Stream, Illinois 60188. All rights reserved. | Scripture quotations marked ESV are from The ESV® Bible (The Holy Bible, English Standard Version®), copyright © 2001 by Crossway, a publishing ministry of Good News Publishers. Used by permission. All rights reserved. | Scripture quotations marked MSG are taken from THE MESSAGE, copyright © 1993, 1994, 1995, 1996, 2000, 2001, 2002 by Eugene H. Peterson. Used by permission of NavPress. All rights reserved. Represented by Tyndale House Publishers, Inc. | Scripture quotations marked NCV are taken from the New Century Version®. Copyright © 2005 by Thomas Nelson. Used by permission. All rights reserved. | Scripture quotations marked NIV are taken from the Holy Bible, New International Version®, NIV®. Copyright © 1973, 1978, 1984, 2011 by Biblica, Inc.™ Used by permission of Zondervan. All rights reserved worldwide. www.zondervan.com. The "NIV" and "New International Version" are trademarks registered in the United States Patent and Trademark Office by Biblica, Inc.™

For foreign and subsidiary rights, contact the author.

Cover design by: Sara Young
Cover photo by: Andrew van Tilborgh

ISBN: 978-1-964794-09-9   1 2 3 4 5 6 7 8 9 10

Printed in the United States of America

INSANELY PRACTICAL LEADERSHIP

STEPHEN BLANDINO

STUDY GUIDE

AVAIL

CONTENTS

Confessions of a Follower 6

CHAPTER 1. HOW TO GROW YOU 10

CHAPTER 2. HOW TO BE A SPIRITUALLY GROUNDED LEADER 18

CHAPTER 3. HOW TO LEAD WITH CHARACTER 24

CHAPTER 4. HOW TO THINK LIKE A LEADER 30

CHAPTER 5. HOW TO MANAGE YOUR TIME 36

CHAPTER 6. HOW TO MAKE LEADERSHIP DECISIONS 42

CHAPTER 7. HOW TO BUILD INFLUENCE 48

CHAPTER 8. HOW TO LEAD PEOPLE 54

CHAPTER 9. HOW TO BE A SERVANT LEADER 60

CHAPTER 10. HOW TO COMMUNICATE WITH PEOPLE 66

CHAPTER 11. HOW TO LEAD THROUGH CONFLICT 72

CHAPTER 12. HOW TO COACH OTHERS 78

"No matter where you are in your leadership journey, this book will help you take the next step."
Mark Batterson, NYT Bestselling Author of *The Circle Maker*

INSANELY PRACTICAL LEADERSHIP

12 NO-NONSENSE KEYS TO MASTER THE ART OF LEADING YOURSELF AND OTHERS

STEPHEN BLANDINO

CONFESSIONS OF A FOLLOWER

> Good leadership is the ability to positively influence people toward a shared vision while maximizing their gifts for the greater good.

READING TIME

As you read "Confessions of a Follower" in *Insanely Practical Leadership*, review, reflect on, and respond to the text by answering the following questions.

REVIEW, REFLECT, AND RESPOND

Do you consider yourself a natural leader or a learned leader?

_____
_____
_____
_____
_____
_____
_____
_____
_____

How does this idea of being a "learned leader" challenge your own perception of what qualifies someone to lead?

_____
_____
_____
_____
_____
_____
_____
_____
_____
_____
_____

Reflect on the leadership failures in this chapter. How have your own mistakes shaped your growth as a leader, and how willing are you to embrace those failures as learning opportunities?

_____
_____
_____
_____
_____
_____
_____
_____
_____
_____

Insecurity can hold you back from accepting advice and suggestions. How does insecurity show up in your leadership, and how might it be limiting your potential?

_____
_____
_____
_____
_____
_____
_____
_____
_____
_____

This chapter emphasizes the value of learning from others and seeking guidance. Who are the key mentors or influences in your life that have helped you grow as a leader? What voices should you be listening to more closely?

_____
_____
_____
_____
_____
_____
_____
_____
_____
_____

CHAPTER 1

HOW TO GROW YOU

> For our dreams to move from hopeful aspirations to vivid reality, we must adopt a growth mindset.

READING TIME

As you read Chapter 1: "How to Grow You" in *Insanely Practical Leadership*, review, reflect on, and respond to the text by answering the following questions.

REVIEW, REFLECT, AND RESPOND

What did you learn about growth from the experience with the editor?

_____
_____
_____
_____
_____
_____

Can you think of a time when you had to sacrifice something (e.g., investing more time, working longer hours, restarting a project from scratch, etc.) to prioritize growth? What was the result?

_____
_____
_____
_____
_____
_____

In what ways have you made personal growth optional? Why?

_____
_____
_____
_____
_____

> "Jesus grew in wisdom and in stature and in favor with God and all the people."
> —Luke 2:52 (NIV)

Consider the scripture above and answer the following questions:

What do you think Jesus did in order to grow in wisdom, stature, and favor with God and people?

_____
_____
_____
_____
_____

In what ways can your personal growth journey mirror that of Jesus's journey?

_____
_____
_____
_____
_____

What are the limitations of relying on natural leadership talents, and how does learned leadership address these gaps?

_____
_____
_____
_____
_____

In what ways might you be relying too heavily on natural leadership abilities, and how is it hindering your ability to maximize your leadership potential?

_____
_____
_____
_____
_____
_____

What role did the mentorship and feedback from the editor play in developing leadership approaches in areas outside of that isolated experience?

_____
_____
_____
_____
_____
_____

What growth lessons have you experienced in one context (e.g., at home, in the workplace, in your relationships) that could be applied to your leadership approach in every area of life?

_____
_____
_____
_____
_____
_____

Consider the **Growth TRAC plan** for pursuing and achieving your growth goals, and develop your own Growth TRAC plan by using the template on the next page:

T (Target)   R (Roadmap)   A (Accountability)   C (Check-up)

	GROWTH QUESTION	GROWTH TRAC
T	**TARGET** What is my growth goal?	Create and cast a compelling vision for my department by May 15.
R	**ROADMAP** What is my growth plan?	<ul><li>Read The Vision Driven Leader by Michael Hyatt.</li><li>Create the first draft of a vision.</li><li>Share the vision with three leaders and make adjustments on two rounds of input.</li><li>Create a vision-casting script and secure feedback from my leadership coach.</li><li>Cast vision to my department.</li></ul>
A	**ACCOUNTABILITY** Who will hold me accountable for my growth?	<ul><li>Accountability Partner: Alan Colson</li><li>Accountability Question: What progress have you made on each step to clarify and cast vision to your department?</li></ul>
C	**CHECK-UP** When and how will I evaluate my growth progress?	Evaluate progress as follows:<ul><li>Read book by January 20</li><li>Create vision draft by February 5</li><li>Secure leadership team input by March 5</li><li>Vision script and coaching by April 15</li><li>Cast vision May 15</li></ul>

	GROWTH QUESTION	GROWTH TRAC
T	**TARGET** What is my growth goal?	
R	**ROADMAP** What is my growth plan?	
A	**ACCOUNTABILITY** Who will hold me accountable for my growth?	
C	**CHECK-UP** When and how will I evaluate my growth progress?	

Why is it essential to form a growth team, and who would you consider inviting to be part of your own team?

_____
_____
_____
_____
_____
_____
_____
_____
_____
_____
_____

What steps can you take to adopt a more disciplined growth mindset in your leadership journey?

_____
_____
_____
_____
_____
_____
_____
_____
_____
_____
_____

What about Karen's education and personal growth story stands out to you? How does it inspire you to take on new challenges in your growth process?

_____
_____
_____
_____
_____
_____
_____
_____
_____
_____
_____
_____

MASTER THE ART

OF LEADING YOURSELF

AND OTHERS

CHAPTER 2

HOW TO BE A SPIRITUALLY GROUNDED LEADER

> Spiritually grounded leaders "expect" God's shaping activity throughout their lives.

READING TIME

As you read Chapter 2: "How to Be a Spiritually Grounded Leader" in *Insanely Practical Leadership*, review, reflect on, and respond to the text by answering the following questions.

REVIEW, REFLECT, AND RESPOND

Reflect on how early prayer and Bible study habits help lay the foundation for spiritual grounding. How have similar practices affected your leadership?

_____
_____
_____
_____
_____

Do you have a "quiet time notebook"? If not, what tools, systems, or habits do you use to cultivate spiritual depth, and how might you improve them?

_____
_____
_____
_____
_____

If someone were to look at your weekly calendar, what would they say about your priorities? What adjustments need to be made?

_____
_____
_____
_____
_____

> "But seek first his kingdom and his righteousness, and all these things will be given to you as well."
> —Matthew 6:33 (NIV)

Consider the scripture above and answer the following questions:

What does it look like to seek the kingdom of God before all things in the day-to-day rhythms of life?

_____
_____
_____
_____
_____
_____
_____
_____

How does this passage challenge the way you are balancing your personal and professional responsibilities right now?

_____
_____
_____
_____
_____
_____
_____
_____

How does this chapter differentiate between spiritual efficiency and spiritual intimacy? What does "unrushed time with God" look like in your life?

_____
_____
_____
_____
_____
_____
_____
_____
_____

Why is there an emphasis on "Jesus must be both first and center"? How does this differ from simply placing Jesus on a checklist of priorities? What internal and external changes do you notice when Jesus becomes a checklist item?

_____
_____
_____
_____
_____
_____
_____
_____
_____

What does it mean to lead at the "pace of prayer"? What does this have to do with effective leadership practices?

___

Reflect on a time when your spiritual grounding was tested. How did your response align with the keys the author suggests for spiritual maturity?

___

How does the perspective on tests and trials (e.g., Joseph's story) inform the way you handle difficulties in leadership? What kind of good might come out of the trials you are facing now? Be specific.

_____
_____
_____
_____
_____
_____
_____

When have you seen God use a challenging time for your good?

_____
_____
_____
_____
_____
_____
_____

What is one specific change you will commit to making in order to become a more spiritually grounded leader?

_____
_____
_____
_____
_____
_____
_____

CHAPTER 3

HOW TO LEAD WITH CHARACTER

> Your example has the power to extend to future generations, but you determine whether it will be one worth following.

READING TIME

As you read Chapter 3: "How to Lead With Character" in *Insanely Practical Leadership*, review, reflect on, and respond to the text by answering the following questions.

REVIEW, REFLECT, AND RESPOND

There's a comparison made between character failures and sinkholes. What character "sinkholes" have emerged from the pressures of your own leadership journey?

_____
_____
_____
_____
_____

What are some warning signs that you might be compromising your values under pressure? How can you address these warning signs before they become bigger issues?

_____
_____
_____
_____
_____

Reflect on a time when your character was tested. How did you respond, and what did you learn from that experience?

_____
_____
_____
_____
_____

> "Don't let anyone look down on you because you are young, but set an example for the believers in speech, in conduct, in love, in faith, and in purity."
> —1 Timothy 4:12 (NIV)

Consider the scripture above and answer the following questions:

How do you personally embody the characteristics mentioned in this verse—speech, conduct, love, faith, and purity—in your leadership role?

_____
_____
_____
_____
_____
_____
_____

In what areas of your leadership could you set a better example for others, as outlined in the scripture?

_____
_____
_____
_____
_____
_____
_____

Think of a leader that you know or used to know who fell. How did it affect you, and how did it change the way you view leadership as a whole?

_____
_____
_____
_____
_____
_____

Consider a time when you were rightly accused of something. What lie did you tell yourself in order to soften the blow? Why does that threaten useful accountability practices and efforts at personal growth?

_____
_____
_____
_____
_____
_____
_____

What values have had the greatest impact on you as a leader? How do you live these out in your leadership?

_____
_____
_____
_____
_____
_____
_____

Who in your life are you accountable to help prevent "sinkholes" in your character? What specific conversations have you had with this person (or group of people) to create a plan for monitoring your character and ensuring you stay aligned with your values?

_____
_____
_____
_____
_____
_____
_____
_____
_____

Reflect on the statement: "Boundaries protect us from ourselves." How do you create boundaries in your leadership, and where might you need to set more?

_____
_____
_____
_____
_____
_____
_____
_____
_____

What do you believe others would say about the ways they see your integrity in action? Provide a specific example.

_____
_____
_____

Do you and your team have a routine practice in place for debriefing and discussing matters of character? If so, how effective are these debriefs? If not, what would this look like for your team?

There's contrasting legacies of King Jeroboam and the apostle Paul. Whose legacy are you building in your leadership? What actions today will create a positive legacy for the future?

CHAPTER 4

HOW TO THINK LIKE A LEADER

> More than anything else, how we think defines who we are, how high we climb, and how well we lead.

READING TIME

As you read Chapter 4: "How to Think Like a Leader" in *Insanely Practical Leadership*, review, reflect on, and respond to the text by answering the following questions.

REVIEW, REFLECT, AND RESPOND

What factors or circumstances have you been attributing your biggest leadership challenges to? In what ways might your thinking be the culprit?

_____
_____
_____
_____
_____

How has a limiting mindset affected your leadership in the past? How are they affecting you now?

_____
_____
_____
_____
_____

Reflect on a recent leadership challenge you faced. How could changing your thinking or perspective have led to a better outcome?

_____
_____
_____
_____
_____
_____

> "Do not conform to the pattern of this world, but be transformed by the renewing of your mind. Then you will be able to test and approve what God's will is—his good, pleasing and perfect will."
> —Romans 12:2 (NIV)

Consider the scripture above and answer the following questions:

What do you think it means to "test and approve" God's will?

_____
_____
_____
_____
_____
_____
_____
_____

Why do you think renewing your mind enables you to test and approve God's will?

_____
_____
_____
_____
_____
_____
_____
_____

Identify three limiting beliefs or thought patterns that are holding you back from effective leadership. What new perspectives or approaches can you adopt to replace them?

_____
_____
_____
_____
_____
_____

"Good leadership requires great thinking."
On a scale of 1 to 5 (1 = very poor to 5 = excellent), how would you rate your effectiveness as a leader? In what ways does your thinking contribute to this rating?

1					2					3					4					5

_____
_____
_____

What might you be overthinking right now as you consider new business initiatives or decisions? How is it impacting your confidence?

_____
_____
_____
_____
_____
_____

Review the list of excuses leaders tend to make. Which ones resonate with you the most?

___

Think of a time when you had a scarcity mindset. How did it impact the people around you? Why do you think scarcity mindsets can have such a ripple effect?

___

It's described that a visionary leader is one who embraces and expects change. Do you see yourself as a visionary? What visions do you have for your team, ministry, or business right now? How do you plan to execute them?

To what extent are your short-term goals taking precedence over your long-term goals?

CHAPTER 5

HOW TO MANAGE YOUR TIME

> Time management doesn't start with time.
> It starts with your purpose and values.

READING TIME

As you read Chapter 5: "How to Manage Your Time" in *Insanely Practical Leadership*, review, reflect on, and respond to the text by answering the following questions.

REVIEW, REFLECT, AND RESPOND

How would you rate your time management skills? What about time management poses the greatest challenge for you?

_____
_____
_____
_____
_____

What habits or distractions in your life waste time and reduce your effectiveness as a leader? What measures can you take to eliminate or reduce these distractions?

_____
_____
_____
_____
_____

Reflect on a time when poor time management led to a missed opportunity. What changes can you make to ensure this doesn't happen again?

_____
_____
_____
_____
_____

> **"Don't waste your time on useless work, mere busywork, the barren pursuits of darkness."**
> **—Ephesians 5:11 (MSG)**

Consider the scripture above and answer the following questions:

What kind of busywork do you find yourself getting caught up in? What do you think is behind this, and who could you outsource this work to?

_____
_____
_____
_____
_____
_____

In this scripture, the "barren pursuits of darkness" refer to sexual immorality, greed, and obscene talk. Have any of these, either in your past or present, hindered or compromised opportunities in your own life? What about in the life of someone you know?

_____
_____
_____
_____
_____
_____

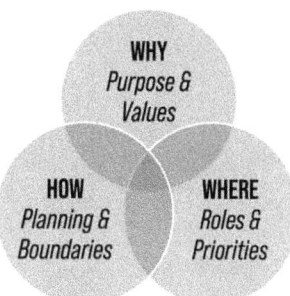

Turn your attention to circle #1 of the diagram (Why: Purpose and Values) shown in this chapter and answer the following questions:

Create a mission statement by answering the "action, audience, and outcome" questions listed in this chapter. How does this help you clarify your purpose?

_____
_____
_____
_____
_____
_____
_____

Identify your values by answering the "people, principles, and priorities" questions listed in this chapter. How do your values and mission complement one another?

_____
_____
_____
_____
_____
_____
_____

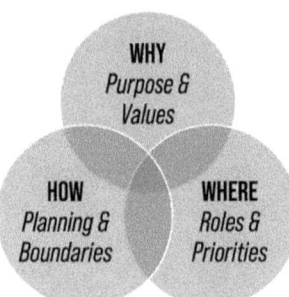

Turn your attention to circle #2 of the diagram (Where: Roles and Priorities) shown in this chapter and answer the following questions:

Which roles (community, campus, church, career, and culture) would your purpose and values be put to use the best?

_____
_____
_____
_____
_____
_____
_____

Which priorities deliver the greatest impact for your roles (required, return, reward)?

_____
_____
_____
_____
_____
_____
_____

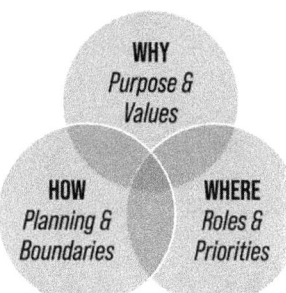

Turn your attention to circle #3 of the diagram (How: Planning and Boundaries) shown in this chapter and answer the following questions:

Which foundational planning practices do you find you struggle with the most?

_____
_____
_____
_____
_____
_____

Out of the listed guardrails for setting boundaries around your time, which have you established and which do you need to establish?

_____
_____
_____
_____
_____
_____

CHAPTER 6

HOW TO MAKE LEADERSHIP DECISIONS

> Lacking wisdom isn't a sin; it's simply the condition we often find ourselves in.

READING TIME

As you read Chapter 6: "How to Make Leadership Decisions" in *Insanely Practical Leadership*, review, reflect on, and respond to the text by answering the following questions.

REVIEW, REFLECT, AND RESPOND

There's emphasis placed on the importance of clarity and conviction in decision-making. Can you recall a leadership decision you made without clarity? What were the consequences, and how could you have approached it differently?

_____
_____
_____
_____
_____
_____
_____
_____

Reflect on a time when you delayed making a decision. How did procrastination impact your leadership and team? What did you learn from that experience?

_____
_____
_____
_____
_____
_____
_____
_____

How do you balance data-driven decision-making with intuition and experience when leading others? Provide examples from your own life.

___

> "If you need wisdom, ask our generous God, and he will give it to you. He will not rebuke you for asking."
>
> —James 1:5

Consider the scripture above and answer the following questions:

How often do you ask God for wisdom when faced with important leadership decisions?

___

In what ways does your decision-making process reflect trust in God's wisdom rather than solely relying on your own understanding?

_____
_____
_____
_____
_____
_____
_____

Making decisions in a timely manner is important. How do you ensure you are making decisions promptly without rushing the process?

_____
_____
_____
_____
_____
_____
_____

How do you navigate decisions that may not have a clear right or wrong answer, and what principles guide you in those moments? Provide an example.

_____
_____
_____
_____
_____
_____
_____

How do you balance the tension between the Decision-Making Dashboard and faith to help you make wise and bold decisions?

_____
_____
_____
_____
_____
_____
_____
_____
_____
_____

Reflect on a time when you received feedback on a decision you made. What kind of feedback did you receive? Did it surprise you? Anger you? Help you? How have you applied it to your work today?

_____
_____
_____
_____
_____
_____
_____
_____
_____
_____

Indecision can lead to stagnation. What areas of your leadership are suffering from indecision, and how can you take steps to move forward?

_____
_____
_____
_____
_____
_____
_____
_____
_____

How does your decision-making style align with the core values of your organization or team?

_____
_____
_____
_____
_____
_____
_____
_____
_____
_____

CHAPTER 7

HOW TO BUILD INFLUENCE

> The real question isn't about how much influence you have, but rather, what will you do with the influence God has entrusted to you?

READING TIME

As you read Chapter 7: "How to Build Influence" in *Insanely Practical Leadership*, review, reflect on, and respond to the text by answering the following questions.

REVIEW, REFLECT, AND RESPOND

When you hear the word "influence," what comes to mind? How effectively do you demonstrate the qualities necessary to build and sustain influence?

_____
_____
_____
_____

In this chapter the importance of trust in building influence is discussed. Reflect on a time when you struggled to gain influence. How might a lack of trust have contributed to this challenge?

_____
_____
_____
_____
_____

In what ways did Paul fulfill the five ingredients needed for influence?

_____
_____
_____
_____
_____

> "Your lives are a letter written in our hearts; everyone can read it and recognize our good work among you. Clearly, you are a letter from Christ showing the result of our ministry among you."
>
> —2 Corinthians 3:2-3

Consider the scripture above and answer the following questions:

In what ways does your life reflect the message of Christ, as if it were a "letter" for others to read? What do you think people "read" about your faith and character through your daily actions?

_____
_____
_____
_____
_____
_____

What do you read in the lives and work of your team that reflects your influence as a leader?

_____
_____
_____
_____
_____
_____

Refer to the influence diagram in this chapter and answer the following questions:

_____
_____
_____
_____
_____
_____
_____
_____

What has God called you to? How has God prepared you for it? How might He be preparing you now?

_____
_____
_____
_____
_____
_____
_____

How wide is your influence? How weighty is your influence?

_____
_____
_____
_____
_____
_____
_____

How are you inspiring others with your vision? How do you know?

_____
_____
_____
_____
_____
_____
_____

Which tips for growing your competence do you find the most helpful?

_____
_____
_____
_____
_____
_____
_____

In what ways have you truly invested in your team?

_____
_____
_____
_____
_____
_____
_____

Reflect on a leader who has greatly influenced you. What qualities did they demonstrate, and how can you adopt similar behaviors to enhance your own influence?

_____
_____
_____
_____
_____
_____
_____
_____

CHAPTER 8

HOW TO LEAD PEOPLE

> **People won't follow you if you can't take them somewhere better or more inspiring than where they are right now.**

READING TIME

As you read Chapter 8: "How to Lead People" in *Insanely Practical Leadership*, review, reflect on, and respond to the text by answering the following questions.

REVIEW, REFLECT, AND RESPOND

Reflect on a time when you failed to meet the needs of your team members. What went wrong, and how can you improve your leadership to better serve them?

_____
_____
_____
_____

Think of a time when task-oriented leadership affected your ability to lead well. What changes did you or can you make to focus more on people?

_____
_____
_____
_____

What stood out to you about Sir Ernest Shackleton's leadership, and what aspects of his story can you apply to the way you lead your team?

_____
_____
_____
_____

> "Care for the flock that God has entrusted to you. Watch over it willingly, not grudgingly—not for what you will get out of it, but because you are eager to serve God. Don't lord it over the people assigned to your care, but lead them by your own good example."
>
> —1 Peter 5:2-3

Consider the scripture above and answer the following questions:

Have you found yourself begrudgingly caring for those you lead? What underlying character or spiritual issues may be contributing to this attitude?

_____

_____

_____

_____

_____

What does it look like, practically, to lord your position over those you care for?

_____

_____

_____

_____

_____

Does your team know the vision for your team, organization, or ministry? What is it, and using the questions listed in the chapter as a guide, how can you communicate it with your team?

_____
_____
_____
_____
_____

What is your strategy for fulfilling the vision? Does it adequately address the five Rs (reality, research, resources, roadmap, and rollout)? How focused and flexible is it?

_____
_____
_____
_____
_____
_____

Consider every person on your leadership team. How clearly have you communicated their roles, and have they established the specific goals associated with their roles?

_____
_____
_____
_____
_____
_____

Review the TREC method (training, resources, experience, coaching) for equipping your team to succeed. Carefully develop a plan to ensure your team has access to all of these components. What gaps or areas for improvement did you identify?

_____
_____
_____
_____
_____
_____
_____
_____

What tasks are you currently handling that could be delegated? Identify these tasks and decide who is best suited to take on each one.

_____
_____
_____
_____
_____
_____

In what ways does your work afford opportunities for collaboration and teamwork? How do you tend to handle divisiveness on your team, and how could you handle it more effectively in the future?

_____
_____
_____
_____
_____

Review the tips listed in the chapter for demonstrating care and compassion for your team. Which of these have you already established as regular habits, and which ones can you start implementing moving forward?

_____
_____
_____
_____
_____
_____
_____
_____
_____
_____

Consider facts, feelings, and frequency as tools for effective communication. How closely do your communication style and practices follow these principles?

_____
_____
_____
_____
_____
_____
_____
_____
_____
_____

CHAPTER 9

HOW TO BE A SERVANT LEADER

> A title should be nothing more than a reminder that you get to serve more people.

READING TIME

As you read Chapter 9: "How to Be a Servant Leader" in *Insanely Practical Leadership*, review, reflect on, and respond to the text by answering the following questions.

REVIEW, REFLECT, AND RESPOND

When was the last time you put the needs of your team above your own ambitions? In what ways are you truly serving others, and in what ways are you more focused on how leadership can serve your own goals?

_____
_____
_____
_____
_____
_____
_____
_____

How often do you actually make sacrifices for those you lead? Identify specific instances where you chose your comfort or convenience over serving your team.

_____
_____
_____
_____
_____
_____
_____
_____

Being a servant leader requires humility. Where are you holding on to pride in your leadership, and how is that pride damaging your relationships and effectiveness?

___

> "I have given you an example to follow. Do as I have done to you. I tell you the truth, slaves are not greater than their master. Nor is the messenger more important than the one who sends the message. Now that you know these things, God will bless you for doing them."
>
> —John 13:15-17

Consider the scripture above and answer the following questions:

As a leader, what would it look like to assume the position of a slave the way Jesus did in submission to His Father?

___

How has God blessed you in the past when you've led with a servant's heart rather than from a position of authority or control?

Servant leadership requires sacrificing personal gain. What comforts, perks, or privileges are you reluctant to give up in order to serve others more effectively?

Are you willing to lead in ways that may never get noticed or praised? How do you handle the tension between wanting recognition and serving with humility?

_____
_____
_____
_____
_____
_____
_____

Who on your team could benefit the most from your time and support right now? Why haven't you already prioritized them, and what steps will you take to change that immediately?

_____
_____
_____
_____
_____
_____
_____
_____
_____

Servant leaders are intentional about developing others. Who are you pouring into on a regular basis? If no one comes to mind, why not?

_____
_____
_____

Servant leadership also demands vulnerability. Where are you hiding behind authority or control to avoid being truly vulnerable with your team?

Which of the seven servant leader choices is lacking in your commitment to be an effective servant leader? What would it look like to put that choice into practice today?

CHAPTER 10

HOW TO COMMUNICATE WITH PEOPLE

> In most cases, poor communication isn't a matter of life and death. And yet, it is.

READING TIME

As you read Chapter 10 "How to Communicate With People" in *Insanely Practical Leadership*, review, reflect on, and respond to the text by answering the following questions.

REVIEW, REFLECT, AND RESPOND

Think about the last time someone on your team misunderstood you. Did you blame them, or did you take responsibility for your lack of clear communication? How can you ensure this doesn't happen again?

_____
_____
_____
_____
_____
_____
_____

Listening is an important part of leadership. How often do you listen to understand rather than to respond? Are you actually hearing your team or just waiting for your turn to speak?

_____
_____
_____
_____
_____
_____
_____

What communication habits have you developed that may be confusing or alienating your team? Are you willing to change them, or are you holding onto them out of habit or ego?

___

> "Words kill, words give life; they're either poison or fruit—you choose."
> —Proverbs 18:21 (MSG)

Consider the scripture above and answer the following questions:

Are your words bringing life or death to those you lead? In what ways have you used your speech to build up or tear down your team?

___

What negative patterns of speech (criticism, sarcasm, impatience) do you need to confront in yourself?

_____
_____
_____
_____
_____
_____
_____
_____
_____
_____

In the chapter it's brought to our attention that body language is a crucial part of communication. How often does your body language undermine the words you're saying? What aspects of your body language could be misinterpreted by your team?

_____
_____
_____
_____
_____
_____
_____
_____
_____
_____

Think about a time when your lack of clarity caused confusion or frustration within your team. How often does this happen, and what are you doing to address it?

_____
_____
_____
_____
_____
_____
_____

Are you truly open to feedback from your team, or do you only want to hear positive affirmations? Why or why not? How does your response to criticism impact your ability to communicate effectively as a leader?

_____
_____
_____
_____
_____
_____
_____

How many of your communication problems stem from assumptions you make about what others understand? How can you challenge yourself to seek clarity before miscommunication spirals into larger issues?

_____
_____
_____

Empathy plays a role in communication. Reflect on team members with whom you have had frustrating interactions or were difficult to work with, and then put yourself in their shoes. How does that change the way you understand those experiences?

How would the TEAM Communication System improve communication in your organization, and which part of the system needs more attention from you?

CHAPTER 11

HOW TO LEAD THROUGH CONFLICT

> The way in which you handle conflict provides an unfiltered picture of your spiritual, emotional, and relational maturity.

READING TIME

As you read Chapter 11: "How to Lead Through Conflict" in *Insanely Practical Leadership*, review, reflect on, and respond to the text by answering the following questions.

REVIEW, REFLECT, AND RESPOND

How often do you avoid conflict in order to keep the peace? What is the real cost of your avoidance, and how is it affecting your team's morale and performance?

_____
_____
_____
_____
_____
_____
_____

Think about a recent conflict you faced. Did you address it head-on, or did you try to soften the blow to avoid tension? How did your approach impact the outcome, and what could you have done differently?

_____
_____
_____
_____
_____
_____
_____

Emotional maturity in conflict is important. Where are you letting your emotions dictate your actions, and how is that undermining your ability to resolve conflict effectively?

___

> "This is how I want you to conduct yourself in these matters. If you enter your place of worship, and, about to make an offering, you suddenly remember a grudge a friend has against you, abandon your offering, leave immediately, go to this friend and make things right. Then, and only then, come back and work things out with God."
>
> —Matthew 5:23-24 (MSG)

Consider the scripture above and answer the following questions:

With whom in your life do you need to make amends or clear the air? What has stopped you, and how will you do it?

___

Why do you think it's important to restore unity with someone before making an offering to God

How often do you let small issues fester until they become bigger problems? What stops you from addressing conflict in its early stages?

Are you more focused on being right during a conflict or on finding a solution that benefits everyone? Provide an example of each. How can you shift your mindset to prioritize resolution over ego?

_____
_____
_____
_____
_____

Unresolved conflict weakens trust. Where is unresolved conflict currently damaging your team's trust in you, and what will you do to start rebuilding that trust?

_____
_____
_____
_____
_____

How do you handle conflict when emotions are running high? In what ways are you leading with a calm, steady hand, and in what ways are you reacting out of frustration or fear?

_____
_____
_____
_____
_____

Think about a recent conflict that didn't end well. What role did you play in that outcome, and how can you take responsibility for your part in ensuring future conflicts are handled better?

_____
_____
_____
_____
_____
_____

Conflict often reveals underlying issues. What deeper problems are you avoiding by not addressing conflict directly, and how can you begin to tackle those root causes?

_____
_____
_____
_____
_____
_____

Which of the six conflict-resolution strategies tends to get the least amount of your attention when you're facing a conflict with someone, and how can you improve in this area?

_____
_____
_____
_____
_____
_____

CHAPTER 12

HOW TO COACH OTHERS

> Coaching isn't just something you need;
> it's also something you should do.

READING TIME

As you read Chapter 12: "How to Coach Others" in *Insanely Practical Leadership*, review, reflect on, and respond to the text by answering the following questions.

REVIEW, REFLECT, AND RESPOND

How much time do you actually spend developing and coaching your team members? If it's less than it should be, what excuses are you making, and how can you start prioritizing their growth?

_____
_____
_____
_____
_____
_____
_____

Think about a time when a team member failed. Did you see it as a coaching opportunity, or did you get frustrated? How can you change your mindset to view failure as a growth opportunity for both you and your team?

_____
_____
_____
_____
_____
_____
_____

Are you allowing yourself to be coached and challenged by others, or are you too focused on being the coach?

Who is coaching you? How are you applying the coaching you receive to the way you coach your team?

It's important to ask the right questions as a coach. How often do you default to giving advice instead of asking probing questions? What can you do to shift your approach and empower others to find their own solutions?

Are you leading in a way that encourages others to grow, or are you stifling development by micromanaging or taking over tasks? How can you give your team more room to grow and take ownership?

How do you handle situations where a team member isn't responding to your coaching efforts? Are you quick to give up, or do you take the time to understand what's really holding them back?

Think about someone on your team who shows great potential but hasn't fully tapped into it yet. What's stopping you from coaching them to reach that potential, and what will you do to help them grow starting now?

___

Coaching requires consistency and follow-through. How often do you let coaching conversations drop after the initial one?

___

Which aspect of the AIM Coaching Model needs greater attention from you in your coaching efforts, and what can you do to provide or encourage better Assessment, Insight, and Movement?

_____
_____
_____
_____
_____
_____
_____
_____
_____
_____

Drawing from the principles and lessons in *Insanely Practical Leadership*, what are three action items you will implement as a leader moving forward?

_____
_____
_____
_____
_____
_____
_____
_____
_____
_____

www.ingramcontent.com/pod-product-compliance
Lightning Source LLC
Chambersburg PA
CBHW062119080426
42734CB00012B/2922